WAY OF THE WATER'S GOING

WAY OF THE

Images of the Northern

TEXT BY

Photographs by

HARPER & ROW, PUBLISHERS • NEW YORK

WATER'S GOING

California Coastal Range

URSULA K. LE GUIN

Ernest Waugh and Alan Nicholson

1817

Grand Rapids, Philadelphia, St. Louis, San Francisco
London, Singapore, Sydney, Tokyo, Toronto

FIRST EDITION

Designed by Cassandra J. Pappas

Library of Congress Cataloging-in-Publication Data

Le Guin, Ursula K., 1929–
   Way of the water's going/text by Ursula K. Le Guin;
photographs by Ernest Waugh and Alan Nicholson.—1st ed.
      p. cm.
   ISBN 0-06-016157-4
   [1. Le Guin, Ursula K., 1929-   Always coming home—
Illustrations.]   I. Waugh, Ernest.   II. Nicholson, Alan.
III. Title.
PS3562.E42A79   1989
813′.54—dc20   89-45050

---

89 90 91 92 93 DT/**HOR** 10 9 8 7 6 5 4 3 2 1

Introduction
by Ursula K. Le Guin

॥॥॥॥॥॥॥॥॥॥॥॥॥॥॥॥॥॥॥॥॥॥॥॥॥॥

When I began to write about the place I have loved the longest, the Napa Valley of Northern California, I found that I wanted to describe it as closely and truly as I could—more closely and truly than is possible: stone by stone. . . . I wanted to know what the stones were, and why these stones—obsidian, hematite, serpentine—were there. I wanted to know and tell the trees and shrubs and grasses native to that stony earth, and the looks and lives of all the creatures that live in the Valley, in its river and creeks, on the wild hills above it and in the air above the hills. When I came to the human inhabitants, however, I deserted history and observation and sought truth another way. I looked for a people who might belong there the way the obsidian, the checkerlily, the acorn woodpecker, and the deer mice belong there: not "masters," not "owners," but true inhabitants, participants, people of the Valley.

Lao Tzu said,

> The spirit of the valley does not die.
> This is the mystery,
> the mother.
>
> The mystery, the mother of the doorway,
> is the root
> of earth and heaven.
>
> Forever this endures, forever.
> And all its uses are easy.

The book I wrote about the Valley is called *Always Coming Home.* The title of this book and the texts that accompany its photographs are taken from it. Some of the texts are descriptions of the landscape, but most are from the literature—stories and poems, written and oral—of the people who might be going to have lived there, the people of the Valley, whom I call the Kesh. If you haven't read that book, a few words or references in the texts may not be clear, but that really doesn't matter; the texts are there to make a word-music that runs with the photographic images, linking and locating and interrelating them.

One of the people in *Always Coming Home,* Flicker the visionary, says in her autobiography:

> Of the vision given me . . . I can tell some parts in
> writing and some I can sing with the drum, but for
> most of it I have not found words or music, though I
> have spent a good part of my life ever since learning
> how to look for them.

Of my "vision" of the Valley, my love for it and knowledge of it, I can tell some parts in writing, but for most of it I too have not found words, though I have spent a good part of my life learning how to look for them.

So when Alan Nicholson and Ernest Waugh first wrote me that they were making a book of photographs for which they wanted to use texts from *Always Coming Home,* I was very curious and interested, but very dubious. One's vision isn't often photographed by somebody else. But when we met (in the Valley, near Sinshan Mountain) I realized a great gift was being offered me. The images I could not speak were there. The vision was there. So we got to work on putting the book together, trying to get everything matched up and flowing in the right direction, "going along easily" as the Kesh would say. It wasn't always easy, but it was always a pleasure for me, because it was true collaboration; we were sharing the vision.

Only a few of the photographs in this book are of the Napa Valley itself. They are of a region of northwestern California which includes the Napa and other "wine valleys." The mountains are those of the Coast Ranges. The counties are Napa, Sonoma, Lake, Mendocino, and Glenn. The area included is the Pacific Coast from about Jenner up to a bit north of Rockport, with a few shots farther south, near San Francisco; south to Napa, north to Round Valley, and east to where the hills come down into the Great Valley of California (with one picture from farther east and north, near Lassen Peak). The peoples who lived in this region before the white conquests were the Coast Miwok, the Pomo, the Wappo, the Wintun, and the Yuki. Being all hill-and-valley it is a diverse and complicated landscape, but climatically, geologically, and ecologically it is quite coherent, and is part of the greater coherence of California—which is not, like some of our states, an arbitrary map delineation, but a real place. Of course, to many—even some who live there—"California" is a myth, a hypester's never-never land. The pictures in this book are not of that oranges–starlets–surfers California; nor are they of the High Sierra familiar in photographs, Muir's Range of Light, though they're nearer that. This California is the place for which Mark Twain's telling adjective was *austere.*

California is isolated to the west by the ocean and to the east and south by terrific deserts and mountain walls. It has continuity only to the north, across the tangle of the Klamaths and the Siskiyous and the lonesome Basin country. It is an ecological island; and so many of its species, as on an island, are native and local: *Vitis californicus,* the wild vine (now the rootstock for every grapevine in the vineyards of the world), the California rose, the California poppy, the California grizzly (extinct), the Valley oak, the digger pine, the redwoods *Sequoia sempervirens* and *Sequoia gigantea,* the madrone, the manzanita—trees as strange to outsiders as the wattle and eucalyptus of Australia which have made themselves splendidly at home in California. The extreme dryness of the summers and of the air is strange to people from the moist east. In the east when grass dies it turns brown, and so people come to the great bare slopes of wild oats in the summer sun and see "brown hills," where a Californian sees pure gold. (Our pictures being black and white, we have neatly evaded this dilemma.)

Those high, bare, round hills, the serpentinite soil where only certain plants can grow, the dwarf forest of the chaparral, the harsh canyons, the torrents of winter that lie bone-dry in summer—it is a strange landscape. It is open and yet secretive. All its uses are easy, and yet it is a land of solitudes and silences. It is rugged but vulnerable, fragile. Austerity describes it, and purity: an essential quality of wilderness. Those who love it feel for it passionately, yearningly, protectively, but with no sense of ownership. This land does not "belong to you and me." It belongs to itself. So Alan Nicholson and Ernest Waugh have seen it, tender, aloof, mysterious—a country still in the Dream Time, half vision, half red dirt.

If you went up from Wakwaha on such a morning you'd come out of the fog somewhere on the road, come right through that roof, and turning, look back on a white fog-sea breaking in brilliant silence on the hills. It has done that for a long time. They are old hills, but fog is older.

Where It Is

5

Around Sinshan Mountain and She Watches and Spring Mountain, hard, dark, depthless silhouettes on the dry sky, the fog comes moistening and blurring and rubbing things out. The mountains all go quietly away. Under a low roof the hills are dim. Every leaf beads and drips.

Where It Is

The roots of the Valley are in wildness, in dreaming, in dying, in eternity. The deer trails there, the footpaths and the wagon tracks, they pick their way around the roots of things. They don't go straight. It can take a lifetime to go thirty miles, and come back.

Where It Is

Whenever I come to this place
always somebody
always somebody
has been walking here before me.

The trails in the grass are thin and crooked,
hard to follow, leading
to the sacred of this place.

On Second Hill

Nobody I asked later, hunters and Bay Lodge people, had ever seen the place I came to on that creek. It was a long, dark pool where the creek seemed to have stopped running. Around the pool grew trees I have not seen anywhere else, with smooth trunks and limbs and triangular, slightly yellow leaves. The water of the pool was speckled and drifted with those leaves. I put my hand into the water and asked it for direction. I felt power in it, and it frightened me.

Stone Telling, I

It was dark and still. It was not the water I knew, not the water I wanted. It was heavy, like blood, and black. I did not drink from it. I squatted there in the hot shade under those trees beside the water and looked for a sign or a word, trying to understand.

Stone Telling, I

It was a rock person, not man or woman, not human, but in shape like a heavy human being, with the blue, blue-green, and black colors and the surfaces of serpentine rock in its skin. It had no hair, and its eyes were lidless and without transparency, seeing very slowly. Serpentine looked at me very slowly with those rock eyes.

The Visionary

Veins stand netted on the bluish boulder
where rain wore the soft rock down.
Blown rain of many winters,
help this soul turn round.

A Meditation in the Eighth House

Dusk had come up onto the mountain before I had found the place I couldn't find, so I had stayed where I was, in a hollow under some manzanita trees. The hollow seemed to shelter me, and manzanitas are pure heyiya. I sat a long time there. . . . Whenever I moved at all, the dry manzanita leaves shouted, "Listen! She's moving!"

Stone Telling, I

A GRASS SONG

Very quietly
this is happening,
this is becoming,
the hills are changing
under the rainclouds,
inside the grey fogs,
the sun going south
and the wind colder,
blowing quietly
from the west and south.
Manyness of rain
falling quietly:
manyness of grass
rising into air.
The hills become green.
This is happening
very quietly.

¶¶¶¶¶¶¶¶¶¶¶¶¶¶¶¶¶¶¶¶¶¶¶¶¶¶¶¶¶¶¶

This is the water,
this is the spring of water
between the dark rocks,
between the blue rocks.

I am at this place now.
I am at the beginning of water.

Ganaiv Wakwana Sinshanshun

The springs of those creeks rise among the rifts of earthquake, among rocks from the floors of seas that were before there were human beings and from the fires inside the earth.

Where It Is

THIS STONE

▯▯▯▯▯▯▯▯▯▯▯▯▯▯▯▯▯▯▯▯▯▯▯▯

He went looking for a road
that doesn't lead to death.
He went looking for that road
and found it.
       It was a stone road.
He walked that road
that doesn't lead to death.
He walked on it awhile
before he stopped,
       having turned to stone.

Not all rocks are equally sensitive. Most basalt doesn't pay attention. It isn't listening. It's still thinking about the fire in the dark, perhaps. Serpentine rock is always sensitive. It's from both the water and fire, it moved and flowed through other rocks to come to the air, and it's always on the point of breaking up, coming apart, turning into dirt. Serpentine listens, and speaks. . . .

In general, rocks aren't living in the same way or at the same pace that we are. But you can find a rock, maybe a big boulder, maybe a little agate in a streambed, and by looking carefully at it, touching it or holding it, listening to it, or by a little talking and singing, a small ceremony, or being still and quiet with it, you can enter into the rock's soul to some extent and the rock can enter into yours, if it's disposed to.

Crows, Geese, Rocks

There was a town called Varred or Berred, on the inside of the northeastern hills. . . . It was somewhere up in the slopes of the very dry hills there, and around the dancing place of that town there were hot springs. . . . People say you can find stonework all along Little Rattlesnake Creek and back up Tongue Draw that's left from their aqueducts.

The Town of Chumo

This creek runs dry among its stones.
Souls of the dead, come drink this water!
Come into this side valley with me,
a restless old woman, unseemly,
troubled, walking on dry grass, dry stones.

The Sun Going South

A SONG USED IN CHUMO WHEN DAMMING A CREEK OR DIVERTING WATER TO A HOLDING TANK FOR IRRIGATION

To the ousel, to the water ousel
may it go, may it go.
Tarweed, the corn roots
need this water also.
Buckbrush, the bean leaves
need this water also.
Way of the water's going,
we do not wish this!
Let it go to the water ousel,
to the waterskater.
Let the wild goose's wings
carry it upward.
Let the dragonfly larva
carry it downward.
We do not wish this,
we do not desire it,
only the water we borrow
on our way to returning.
We who are doing this
all will be dying.
Way of the water's going,
bear with us in this place now
on your way to returning.

When we were in the golden hills northeast of Clear Lake, lying down to sleep on the third night, I began to feel the Valley behind me like a body, my own body. My feet were the sea-channels of the River, the organs and passages of my body were the places and streams and my bones the rocks and my head was the Mountain.

Stone Telling, II

UNDER KAIBI

▥▥▥▥▥▥▥▥▥▥▥▥▥▥▥▥▥▥▥▥

How the water winds slowly, slowly
in the mudflats, in the fog,
on the low dim levels.
A sound of long wings,
but I cannot see the heron.

‖‖‖‖‖‖‖‖‖‖‖‖‖‖‖‖‖‖‖‖‖‖‖‖‖‖‖‖‖‖

The shining unsleeping strangers!
The people of the deep waters!
May they be released,
let them return to the south wind,
let them return to the west wind,
let them come to the Valley,
the cloud people, the rainclouds,
send them, O sea, release them,
as the hills send down the creeks,
as the River descends to you,
as our singing descends to you,
as we dance down to you,
releasing, returning the waters,
the turning of river and rainfall,
the sea to the source returning.

Dry Time Invocation

44

We speak as if to a person, saying, "Heya!" to a stone, saying to the sun rising, "Heya! Holy! I greet you!" We cry out as if to a person when alone in the wilderness we cry, "Bless me as I bless you, help me in my weakness!" Whom do we greet? Whom do we bless? Who helps?

Maybe in all things there is one person, one spirit whom we greet in the rock and the sun and trust in all things to bless and help. . . .

...**M**aybe the oneness of the universe manifests that one spirit and the oneness of each being of the many kinds is a sign or symbol of that one person. Maybe so. People who say it is so call that person the self of all selves or the other of all others, the one eternal, the god. The lazyminded may say that inside the rock a spirit lives, inside the sun a fiery person lives, but these say that in the universe the god lives as a human lives in a house or a coyote in the wilderness, having made it, keeping it in order. These people believe. They are not lazy-minded. . . .

. . . **S**ome other people are better at thinking than at believing, and they wonder and ask who it is that we greet, that we bless, that we ask for blessing. Is it the rock itself, the sun itself, all things in themselves? Maybe so. After all, we live in this house which makes itself and keeps itself. Why should a soul be afraid in its own house? There are no strangers. The walls are life, the doors are death; we go in and out at our work.

I think it is one another whom we greet, and bless, and help. It is one another whom we eat. We are gatherer and gathered. Building and unbuilding, we make and are unmade; giving birth and killing, we take hands and let go.

Person and Self

All there under the water are cities, the old
  cities.

All the bottom of the sea there is roads and
  houses,
        streets and houses.

Under the mud in the dark of the sea there
        books are, bones are.

All those old souls are under the sea there,
        under the water, in the mud,
        in the old cities in the dark.

There are too many souls there.

The Inland Sea

The sands of all the beaches of all the coasts, the sand of all the beaches of all the coasts of all the world, are the lives of the unborn, who will be born, who may be born. . . .

. . . The waves of the sea, the bubbles of foam of the waves that break on the coasts of the seas of the world. . . .

. . . all the flashes and gleams of light on the waves of the seas of the world, the flicker of sunlight on waves of the ocean, those are the lives of the Nine Houses of Life without end vanishing without stay forever.

The Day After the World

Adobe, blue clay, serpentine, obsidian:
floors and walls
of the houses of the town of earth.
Cloud, rain, wind, air:
windows and roofs
of the houses of the town of earth.

The Town of Earth

The Inland Sea along that coast is very shallow, crowded with sandbars and islands, and on those islands is where they grow the cotton. . . . We had to get into one of their boats, flat things that felt very unsafe, and go out to the most important island.

Trouble with the Cotton People

It was always an austere land, generous but not lush, not soft, not gentle. It always had two seasons: one wet, one dry. . . . The turn from one season to the other is less transition than reversal. A few dark-grey, pouring days when the burnt and sodden brown hills brighten suddenly into the aching, piercing green of the new grass. . . . A few cloud-flurried, shining days when the orange poppies, the blue lupine, the vetch, clover, wild lilac, brodiaea, blue-eyed grass, daisies, lilies are all in bloom, whole hillsides white and purple and blue and gold, but at the same moment the grass is drying, turning pale, and the wild oats have already sown their seed. Those are the times of change: the greening into winter, the dying into summer.

Where It Is

The chaparral is like atoms and the components of atoms: it evades. It is innumerable. It is not accidentally but essentially messy. . . . This thing is nothing to do with us. This thing is wilderness. The civilized human mind's relation to it is imprecise, fortuitous, and full of risk. . . . The mind can imagine that shadow of a few leaves falling in the wilderness; the mind is a wonderful thing. But what about the shadows of all the other leaves on all the other branches on all the other scrub oaks on all the other ridges of all the wilderness? If you could imagine those even for a moment, what good would it do? Infinite good.

Pandora Finds a Way

Everything that came to me I spoke to by name or by saying heya, the trees, fir and digger pine and buckeye and redwood and manzanita and madrone and oak, the birds, blue jay and bushtit and wood-pecker and phoebe and hawk, the leaves of cham-ise and scrub oak and poison oak and flowering thorn, the grasses, a deer's skull, a rabbit's drop-pings, the wind blowing from the sea.

Stone Telling, I

TO THE PEOPLE ON THE HILLS

On four feet, on four feet walking
around the world, walking around
on four feet, you walk
the right way, you walk dancing,
beautifully dancing you walk,
carefully, dangerously you walk
in the right direction.

PUMA DANCE

I put down my southwest foot,
four round toes, one round pad,
in the dirt by the digger pine,
in the dust by the digger pine
          on the mountain.

I put down my northwest foot,
four round toes, one round pad,
in the dirt by the bay laurel,
in the dust by the bay laurel
          in the foothills.

I put down my northeast foot,
four round toes, one round pad,
in the dirt by the madrone,
in the dust by the madrone
          on the mountain.

I put down my southeast foot,
four round toes, one round pad,
in the dirt by the live oak,
in the dust by the live oak
          in the foothills.

I am standing in the middle
of the lion world
on the mountain of the lion,
in the hills of the lion.
I am standing in the tracks of the lion.

CLOUDS, RAIN, AND WIND

|||||||||||||||||||||||||||||||||||||||

From the house of the Lion that lies on the
  mountain,
footsteps of the dancers approaching,
hurrying: listen, the footsteps
of Bear dancers hurrying downwards
over the foothills towards us.
Coyote, Coyote follows them,
        Coyote howling and singing!

To dance the dancing:
shining, shining.

In the houses
they are dancing.
On the dancing places
they are dancing shining.

The Gyres

In the morning I would come outdoors at sunrise. All beyond and below the porch of that house I would see a vast pluming blankness, the summer fog filling the Valley, while the first rays of the sun brightened the rocks of the Mountain's peaks above me. I would sing as I had been taught:

> "It is the valley of the puma,
> where the lion walks,
> where the lion wakes,
> shining, shining in the Seventh
>   House!"

Later, in the rainy season, the puma walked on the Mountain itself, darkening the summits and the springs in cloud and grey mist. To wake in the silence of that rainless, all-concealing fog was to wake to dream, to breathe the lion's breath.

The Visionary

If the people of the Valley took the City of Mind for granted as a "natural thing," as we would say, the City itself seemed to recognise its ancient origins in human artifacts by the TOK word for the human species and its members, which translates as "makers."

The City

Great Valley oaks stood along the sides of the road to give windbreak and shade, and in places elms, or poplars, or huge white eucalyptus so vast and twisted that they looked older than the Road.

Stone Telling, I

Then we went on a little way and we came to the Line. It smells like some kinds of soap and also like something burnt. It is like a very wide ladder lying on the ground that comes from so far away in the northwest and so far away in the southeast that you can't see either end. On both sides of it the grass is all cut down and there are beautiful smooth rocks inside it. We went across it by stepping on one of the rungs. We went up on a hill with thistles and under some oaks we sat down and ate some pickles and eggs. While we were there there was a noise far away like a drum.

The Train

When I take you to the Valley, you'll see the blue hills on the left and the blue hills on the right, the rainbow and the vineyards under the rainbow late in the rainy season, and maybe you'll say, "There it is, that's it!" But I'll say, "A little farther." We'll go on, I hope, and you'll see the roofs of the little towns and the hillsides yellow with wild oats, a buzzard soaring and a woman singing by the shallows of a creek in the dry season, and maybe you'll say, "Let's stop here, this is it!" But I'll say, "A little farther yet." We'll go on, and you'll hear the quail calling on the mountain by the springs of the river, and looking back you'll see the river running downward through the wild hills behind, below, and you'll say, "Isn't that it, the Valley?" And all I will be able to say is, "Drink this water of the spring, rest here awhile, we have a long way yet to go, and I can't go without you."

Pandora Gently to the Gentle Reader

When the sun turned south the dancers and riders came again from Chukulmas to Telina, and I rode in the games and races, spending all day and night at the fields. People said, "That girl is in love with the roan stallion from Chukulmas," and teased me about it, but not shamefully; everybody knows how adolescents fall in love with horses, and songs have been made about that love. But the horse knew what was wrong; he would no longer let me handle him.

The Visionary

Singing and doing heyiya all day long in the town that was empty and open, I began to feel my soul opening out and spreading out with the other souls of the dancers to fill the emptiness. The water poured out from the bowl of blue clay, and the songs were streams and pools in the great heat of summer. The other Houses came in from the summering, and we danced the Water. . . . On the last night the balconies were full of people . . . and in the sky the heat lightning danced in the southeast and the northwest, and you could not tell the drums from the thunder, and we danced the Rain down to the sea and up to the clouds again.

Stone Telling, I

L isten, you people of the Adobes, you people of
  the Obsidian!
Listen, you gardeners and farmers, orcharders and
  vintners, shepherds and drovers!
Your arts are admirable and generous, arts of
  plenty and increase, and they are dangerous.
Among the tasselled corn the man says, this is my
  plowing and sowing, this is my land.
Among the grazing sheep the woman says, these
  are my breeding and caring, these are my sheep.
In the furrow the seed sprouts hunger.
In the fenced pasture the cow calves fear.
The granary is heaped full with poverty.
The foal of the bridled mare is anger.
The fruit of the olive is war.
Take care, you Adobe people, you Obsidian
  people, and come over onto the wild side,
don't stay all the time on the farming side; it's
  dangerous to live there.
Come among the unsown grasses bearing richly,
      the oaks heavy with acorns, the sweet
      roots in unplowed earth.

An Exhortation to the Second and Third Houses of the Earth

86

Have I burned all the libraries of Babel?

Was it I that burned them?

If they burn, it will be all of us that burned them. But now while I write this they aren't burnt; the books are on the shelves and all the electronic brains are full of memories. Nothing is lost, nothing is forgotten, and everything is in little bits.

Pandora Worrying

Coyote went on and goes along, hunting live things, eating dead things. Coyote is not life or death, but only Coyote.

Owl, Coyote, Soul

Don't break your handbones
trying to break mystery.
Pick it up, eat it, use it, wear it,
throw it at coyotes.

The bones of your heart,
there's mystery.
Clothes wearing the body,
there's a good clown.

Bone Poems

The solution
dissolves itself
leaving the problem behind,
a skeleton,
the mystery before,
around, above, below, within.
O Clarity!

Bone Poems

Well, ways always change. They never stay the same, even when they're very good ways, very beautiful, like that house, you know. They stopped building like that, but then maybe somebody else does it, in another time, another place. . . ."

Time and the City

Ounmalin, Ounmalin!
Beautiful on the River!
To the barns under the dark oaks
the cattle return at evening.
The sound of their cowbells
is like the ringing of water.

Dragonfly Song

From the round hill over Ounmalin
one can see all the vineyards,
and hear the people singing,
coming from the vineyards home at evening.

Dragonfly Song

We live in the low places
like water and shadows.
Our houses do not last long.
We have lost sight behind us
of the spiritual Tower.
We go on down along the river.

The High Tower

THE VALLEY OAK

No one has built
so beautiful
a house as this
great heyimas
deep-towering.

Puzzlebits make whole puzzles.
Answers complete questions.
A whistle, though,
made from the heartbone,
plays the song the crow knows
and won't sing,
the song called Rejoining.

Bone Poems

In late sunshine I wander troubled.
Restless I walk in autumn sunlight.
Too many changes, partings, and deaths.
Doors have closed that were always open.
Trees that held the sky up are cut down.

The Sun Going South

Ballround, earth-town.
Each street meets
itself at length.
Old are the roads,
long are the ways,
wide are the waters.
Whale swims west returning east,
tern flies north returning south,
rain falls to rise, sparks rise to fall.
Mind may hold the whole,
but on foot walking we do not come
to the beginning end of the street.
The hills are steep,
the years are steep,
deep are the waters.
In the round town
it is a long way home.

Teaching Songs

How could it begin once only? That doesn't seem sensible. Things must have ended and begun again, so that it can go on, the way people live and die, all the people, the stars also.

Four Beginnings

They walked softly here. So will the others, the ones I seek.

The only way I can think to find them, the only archaeology that might be practical, is as follows: You take your child or grandchild in your arms, or borrow a young baby, not a year old yet, and go down into the wild oats in the field below the barn. Stand under the oak on the last slope of the hill, facing the creek. Stand quietly. Perhaps the baby will see something, or hear a voice, or speak to somebody there, somebody from home.

Towards an Archaeology of the Future

Rock was softer than the rain,
tree weaker than the worm. No help for it.
So soul be weak, fail, drift, and blow
with wind through net and maze, and sing
one note once only in the wilderness.

A Meditation in the Eighth House

From their houses, from their town
rainbow people come walking. . . .

They climb the ladders of wind,
the stairways of cloud.
They descend the ladders of air,
the steps of rain falling.
The closed eye sees them.
The deaf ear hears them.
The still mouth speaks to them.
The still hand touches them.
Going to sleep we waken to them,
walking the ways of their town.
Dying we live them,
entering their beautiful houses.

A Madrone Lodge Song

Of the vision given me in the Ninth House I can tell some parts in writing, and some I can sing with the drum, but for most of it I have not found words or music, though I have spent a good part of my life ever since learning how to look for them.

The Visionary

It was the universe of power. It was the network, field, and lines of the energies of all the beings, stars and galaxies of stars, worlds, animals, minds, nerves, dust, the lace and foam of vibration that is being itself, all interconnected, every part part of another part and the whole part of each part, and so comprehensible to itself only as a whole, boundless and unclosed.

The Visionary

I would go to sleep and then be partly awake again, perceiving. . . . Near the creek I began to feel the big, deep roots of trees, and in the dirt everywhere the fine, many roots of the grasses, the bulbs of brodiaea and blue-eyed grass, the ground squirrel's heart beating, the mole asleep. I began to come up one of the great roots of a buckeye, up inside the trunk and out the leafless branches to the ends of the small outmost branches. From there I perceived the ladders of rain. These I climbed to the stairways of cloud. These I climbed to the paths of wind. There I stopped. . . .

The Visionary

Afterword by Alan Nicholson

Where do we come from and where are we going? If you look at the faces of people walking on a city street you will see that basically people have a lot in common; they're all much the same in many ways. Yet their faces and gestures and outward clothing describe differences— individuality. Although their nature is the same, each expression of this nature is different. In the same way, things in the natural environment— trees, stones, mountains—although essentially all from the same source, are each different expressions of nature. I'm not interested in portraiture. I have a very difficult time capturing the essence of a personal soul, but I feel sensitive to the soul of a peopleless landscape and the different nuances of expression landscape can provide.

But these nuances are not important because they're referential. My pictures of trees are not about trees, they're about making a good photograph. They're about composition. They're about making the most powerful image possible. Most of all, they're about light. Everything is relevant to light. It's one of the great polarities, light and dark, like life and death. Light is all pervasive. After all, it's only the degree of light present that gives us detail, shadow, those nuances of difference in the landscape. What we think of as landscape is generated out of powerful polarities: heat and cold, dryness and wetness, light and dark. We know each member in the polarity because of the presence of the other. Light defines dark and vice versa. My interest in this polarity has led me to seek strong contrast in my work. I feel that images that dramatize this opposition through strong graphic qualities are more timeless and have more strength.

I seek outward for a set of circumstances that can afford artistic vision, but I also need to locate an inner connection to establish my own place in the landscape and personal relation to it. So I also try to express my own mood, something that clicks, something that unites the self with the world outside so that there's a bonding of the self to the landscape.

Photography is about visual imagery and visual imagery doesn't really have a language; its language is light. Good art takes something the individual sees and makes it something for everybody to remember; the familiar has to become archetypal, has to respond to the inner yearning in the viewer for the transcendent or meaningful.

The quality I'm looking for in an image is dependent on compositional content, on relationships of positive and negative space, on the contrast between light and dark, and on strong compositional ideas. I don't care much about technical qualities like resolution, for example. So the camera makes little difference. I'm sometimes more at home with a funky "soft-at-the edges" old camera than with an expensive high-tech camera with a modern, coated high-resolution lens. To me, the equipment isn't as important as the eye and the mind looking through the equipment.

I've never held the darkroom to be too important either. It's rewarding to develop the film and print the negative and produce a finished image, but that rarely matches the elation one gets from creating the latent image in the field—the experience of getting out there and searching in a state of heightened awareness.

Arriving at that image in the field is partly the result of making and partly the result of discovering. You place the tripod somewhere and start honing in on a particular set of compositional happenings that you have discovered. But at the same time, you begin to visualize or "make up" what can be done with these. You're ensconced in a kind of psychic high during this process—a heightened sense of awareness—until the creative process takes over and translates the euphoria into an image.

But what attracts me to a particular area? It's a subjective apprehension of the sacral—perhaps light and shadow reflected off formations in the landscape, combinations of water, earth, stone, or clouds. And this sacrality is like a power point, with a particular, notable energy, almost a place of healing energy, or power, which is different from that emanating from the surrounding area.

You never know whether this is just a psychological need or a metaphorical symbol (in psychological terms), or whether there truly *is* an energy there in the land. A lot of the appeal of going out and connecting with a landscape that is away from people and away from machinery and man-made stimulation is that one gets a feeling of this life pulse, this animism, not only from animate subjects but also from inanimate objects. Some people may scoff at the idea that animals communicate with one another or even more that there is an active being present in rocks and hills, or that streams or rivers might have spirits. But I feel that is a reality, an extended or parallel world that most people aren't aware of. As long as man has been here, at least a part of mankind has been worshipping the spirit behind the sun and stars and water. Some of us have held these elements sacred and close to our hearts. Others have plundered and neglected this world.

There's a great shared feeling between Ursula's work and ours for a world we live in—for the spirit not only of living things but of inanimate objects, the world, the cosmos, and our place in it—how rocks are the stones that make up the earth we live on, and how they have their own being, in a way, as living things have their being. They've been here longer than we have and will be here longer than we will. Ursula has pointed out, elsewhere, that even the youngest rock is far older than any species that can pick it up and skip it across a pond* and somehow I'd like to emphasize the importance of that. It speaks of something more permanent than we are. It is a wonderful thought to live with.

Part of the attraction of photography is gadgets and mechanical doodads, but on a more real level, it's feeling the wind, and getting out and sticking your toes in the creek, and climbing a hill and getting sweaty. Sometimes I hop in my truck loaded down with cameras and bags of film and zoom down the highway looking for the best pastry outlet in some distant town, and that, too, is part of the appeal. I've found photography both an exhilarating way to release energy and a way to give myself strength. It also gives me a way to relate to the larger world of day to day. It's exciting to put your mind in a receptive attitude toward your environment and become aware of how the elements around you are changing.

Actually, of the three of us, I'm the one who feels somewhat like an urban refugee where I live and photograph. Yet it is nice to be able to walk out to the wilderness within minutes, to be able to see rabbits cross the street and hear birds chirp and coyotes howl. But really, I feel one ought to be able to photograph anywhere. In the same way that cameras are not important to me, the location I'm photographing in is not of primary importance.

On the other hand, I do have a difficult time sometimes—say if I go to the coast or the central valley—places I'm familiar with but not closely familiar with—I do have a difficult time photographing them sometimes. It is possible to walk out your back door and start photographing without having to make a major trip out of connecting with what's there. For example, *From Babylon* (page 109) was taken near my back door. In your own backyard you're not distracted from the creative process. You become more sensitive to nuances in the landscape—what works and what

* *Buffalo Gals* (Santa Barbara: Capra Press, 1987), p. 55.

doesn't work. If it didn't work last week, you can return and see what changes next week. *Light Harvest: Metal Vineyard* (page 87) was a product of many visits over a several week period recording changes in light and atmosphere.

If we ask ourselves why we make art, it's not fundamentally to solve artistic problems, though as I've said, that is an important part of what creative moments are about. But it's so that we can affirm our vision of life.

ALAN NICHOLSON

Afterword by Ernest Waugh

I turned to photography from writing when I ran out of things to say. It was my wife's idea to give me something to do. I'd played with cameras and darkroom equipment since I was a boy, but never for aesthetic reasons, and when I began to do so I was delighted. One experience I always valued in writing was getting to see how the story line would finish and how the whole work would look in its entirety. The problem was, if the work was a story, I would have to wait two months to experience this "completeness," and if I were working on a novel it might take two years, and this was frustrating, and if the work didn't jell, that was devastating.

Taking pictures, I suddenly realized that I was executing entire works in, oh, say, an eighth of a second on a cloudy day with slow film! And after a quarter of an hour in the darkroom, I'd have a pilot print that would show me the work, resolved and entire, for better or for worse. Shooting six-by-six frames on 120 film, I could see twelve works manifest at one time out of the developing tank!

I use a lot of old cameras, especially old folding-bellows cameras. I'm interested in the images the older lenses produce, including distortions of one kind or another. In our present era of contrasty lenses, hard papers, high-contrast developers and film, the lower-contrast lenses of yesterday can provide some balance.

I also turn to the older viewfinder cameras when I want more indefinite framing. Basically, framing is what you leave in and what you leave out at the edge of the picture. When I want to define that picture edge very exactly, I use a reflex camera. But sometimes, I want to be looser and operate more intuitively and with more of a sense of discovery. And at those times I turn to the viewfinder cameras.

Another reason I use old cameras is harder to explain. The fact that these cumbersome old machines are often obstacles to picture taking actually makes me more aware of what I'm doing when I'm taking a picture. In some states of mind, the fact that I'm using an artifact to produce an artifact makes the process more meaningful.

Many of the pictures in this book are taken with these cameras. The picture *Valley Oaks* (page 105), for example, was taken with a Kodak Autographic 3A that my grandfather used to do surveying in the Sierras in the teens of this century. I modified it to take 120 film. *Guidiville* (page 9) was taken with a Balda that my father brought back from Germany after World War II.

Not all my old cameras are cumbersome either. Many of the pictures in this book were taken with a scale-focusing Voigtlander Perkeo given to me by Anne Lohrli. This camera takes 120 film, is light, accurate, and easier to use than most 35-mm cameras.

The art of photography depends on the technology of photography, which is intriguing but also troublesome. In this respect, an art like writing is much freer; if you have a pencil and paper you can write. If you're a photographer, you depend on several machines and chemicals and the dependency can be quite particular and exacting. During the time that I was doing pictures like *Cliff Dwelling* and *Dry Creek* (pages 35, 37), I had developed a very carefully orchestrated technological routine that worked very well but depended on certain *things*. I would radically underexpose the negatives, using Kodak Verichrome Pan or Agfa Pan 25, and then develop the film in Agfa Atomol to produce very, very thin negatives with no blocked highlights and very fine resolution. Then I would print on hard paper, grade 4, and use Selektol as well as Dektol in the paper developer—and I *had it down.* Suddenly Atomol was no longer available! "But wait a minute," I wanted to say, "my work depends on that stuff!" So what?! It took me a year and a half to come up with another routine relying on a new set of chemicals and paper to produce results that are, in their own but different way, just as satisfying to me. But the new formula required changing everything I did, right back to the exposure I used in taking the picture. Photography is full of stories like that.

"Photography," someone once said, "can be reduced to one idea: follow the directions on the box!" Doesn't matter what the box is: camera, film box, enlarger, developer, whatever. I suspect that one could go an astonishing distance with this simple, lucid principle. After all, who knows more about what to do with Verichrome Pan than Kodak chemists, and they tell you what to do on the box! So why does no one that I know, including myself, follow this principle? For one thing the box might disappear, as in my Atomol story. For another thing, all photographers, whether in the field or in the darkroom, want to reach for effects that are just beyond what is prescribed, guaranteed, or designated.

Printing, for me, is part of the art of photography. It is an interpretive and expressive act in itself. We chose Edward Dyba, a master printer, to reprint our negatives for this book, and in some instances he printed my pictures quite differently than I would. His own strong, interpretive sense has left its indelible stamp on this collection, and so the pictures here are not just Alan's and mine, but partly Eddie's too.

The foregoing rests on the assumption that what we're doing when we're taking pictures is "doing art." But my intentions are more varied. Sometimes my intentions are artistic, and I've come a little way with this kind of picture. I now know when I look in the finder if I'm going to get something good. This works infallibly at least for the second rank of pictures I produce. The best still seem to require some chaos and confusion.

Sometimes, though, I have other intentions. I may see an object or even a light effect that fascinates me, and merely want to take home a souvenir. I call that intention "documentary," probably in an attempt to ennoble it. *Bo's Tree* (page 115) is such a picture. My intention was merely to take home a recording of a fascinating sight. Years of evolving prints have, I hope, turned an artifact into a work of art, but it wasn't initially intended as art.

I have another intention in taking some pictures, which I call "metaphysical." The act of taking these pictures makes me more awake to the environment and to myself than I would be otherwise. Taking these pictures is a kind of spiritual experience, and the experience is almost always more significant than the artifact printed later. *Oak Clump and Buckeye* (page 125) is an example of such a picture. I was so uninterested in the result that I didn't even bother to look at it on the proof sheet. It took Andy Vagt to point out to me that it was the best thing there.

There is a spiritual dimension to *Always Coming Home,* and there is a spiritual dimension to Alan's photographs and my photographs and to our lives. We both live with our families in a Buddhist community and have made Buddhist practices a part of our lives and a part of our work.

People who become bored with landscape have asked me if I do other kinds of work. I've done some product work; I've done some portraits. I like doing portraits when I have the occasional knack and when the person is a person I want to photograph. I'm a terrible candid photographer; I did a wedding once, and the slides were so bad I couldn't give them away. I have the greatest respect for photojournalists and for photojournalists who are also great artists, like W. Eugene Smith. When we were visiting Eddie Dyba's studio in San Francisco, a young man who had just returned from a photographic mission in El Salvador was standing at the counter. Who could not but admire the courage and the political commitment involved in that work of documenting human suffering? But

I don't do good candid work. I do landscape. And I don't think landscape is a trivial concern.

The land in which we live—the hill and valley country of Northern California—forms the very special content of the pictures in this book. As this land is also the environment of *Always Coming Home*, I won't try to describe it in words, since Ursula Le Guin's text, included with our pictures, does this magnificently. I can say a little in general. It is a wonderful landscape, wild and domestic, gentle and stark—unique. It is attended with a wonderful light, warmer than the coastal light, less brilliant than the light of the eastern Sierra, soft and radiant. I feel a special debt to the countryside that afforded us the experience of producing this book, particularly as it is disappearing fast. I have been afraid to return to the site of *Hough Springs* 1 (page 71), which was taken before the great fires of September '87—I'm afraid that that hillside will no longer be there. And the freeways and the logging are changing the landscape faster than the fires can.

I feel a special debt also to *Always Coming Home* and to Ursula Le Guin. I am an avid reader of science fiction, and Ursula Le Guin is one of our greatest science fiction writers. And so, when Kathleen McKenna told me that Ursula had written a book set generally in the area in which we live, I was very excited and eager to read it. What I discovered was a book that is great indeed, but *not,* really, at all a book of science fiction. I won't try to tell you what kind of a book I think it is. The texts that accompany our pictures will give you a clear, if partial, sense of the whole. For those of you who have already read *Always Coming Home,* I hope you will find this book a complementary experience. For those who have not read *Always Coming Home,* I hope this book will persuade you to read it. It was a full seven months after reading *Always Coming Home* that the idea of matching the text with our pictures occurred to me. I won't tell you why; that should all be apparent.

Alan joins me in thanking Ursula Le Guin personally for her generosity, her creativity, her patience, and her incredible energy! This work would be impossible without her and *Always Coming Home.* We also want to thank Edward Dyba, our printer. And Alan wants to thank his wife, Terry Nicholson. I also want to thank my mother, Elizabeth Waugh, Anne Lohrli, Stan and Toni Shoptaugh, Kathleen McKenna, Andy and Terry Vagt, and my wife, Barbara, all people without whom this work would not have been possible.

ERNEST WAUGH

133

PHOTOGRAPHS BY ALAN NICHOLSON

PHOTOGRAPHS BY ERNEST WAUGH

Ursula K. Le Guin was born and raised in Northern California, and it is a place she goes back to frequently. A resident of Portland, Oregon, where her husband teaches at Portland State University, Le Guin has been a writer of outstanding fiction for many years and has earned a reputation as one of America's most accomplished and admired novelists. Her novels include *The Lathe of Heaven, The Left Hand of Darkness, The Dispossessed, Orsinian Tales, The Beginning Place,* and *Always Coming Home.* She has twice been a finalist for the National Book Award in fiction, and she has won both the Nebula and Hugo Awards for her science fiction. She is also the author of several collections of short stories, poetry, criticism, screenplays, and a book of essays, *Dancing at the Edge of the World.*

As an author of books for children, she has won the National Book Award, the Newberry Medal, and the Globe-Hornbook Award for juvenile fiction.